OUR BEST SCRAP QUILTS

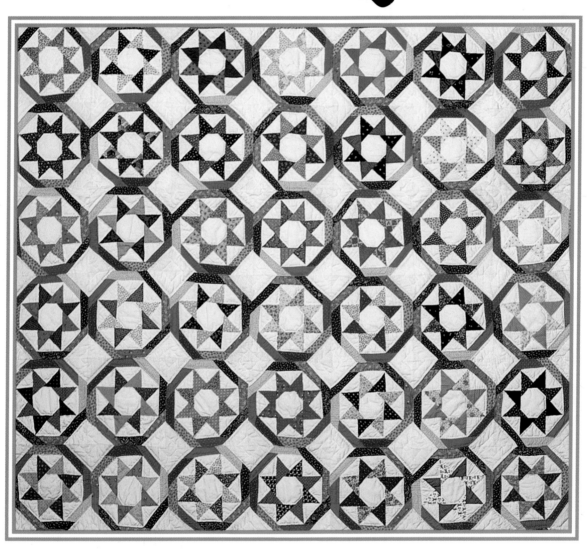

Contents

OUR BEST SCRAP QUILTS

©1994 by Oxmoor House, Inc.

Book Division of Southern Progress Corporation
P.O. Box 2463, Birmingham, AL 35201

Published by Oxmoor House, Inc., and
Leisure Arts, Inc.

Library of Congress Catalog Number: 94-69238
ISBN: 0-8487-1262-5

Manufactured in the United States of America
Second Printing 1995

Editor-in-Chief: Nancy Fitzpatrick Wyatt
Editorial Director, Special Interest Publications:
  Ann H. Harvey
Senior Crafts Editor: Susan Ramey Cleveland
Senior Editor, Editorial Services: Olivia Kindig Wells
Art Director: James Boone

OUR BEST SCRAP QUILTS

Editor: Carol Cook Hagood
Editorial Assistant: Adrienne E. Short
Copy Editor: Susan Smith Cheatham
Production and Distribution Manager: Phillip Lee
Production Manager: Gail H. Morris
Associate Production Manager: Theresa L. Beste
Production Assistant: Marianne Jordan Wilson
Design Concept: Larry Hunter
Design Layout/Illustrations: Carol Loria
Patterns and Illustrations: Kelly Davis
Publishing Systems Administrator: Rick Tucker
Senior Photographer: John O'Hagan
Photostylist: Katie Stoddard

Dear Quilting Friends,

To my grandma, and perhaps to yours as well, the words scrap and quilt were synonymous. All her quilts came from her scrap bag—pieces left over from clothes she made for her family, salvaged sections of her husband's worn-out shirts, carefully washed and pressed print flour sacks and feed sacks. Buying yard goods for the express purpose of making quilts was unheard of in my grandma's circle.

Although today's quilters usually aren't limited to leftovers, the tradition of the scrap quilt lives on. In this book, you'll find examples spanning some 130 years—from Jennifer Rozens's *Evening Star* made from her great-grandmother's blocks to Anna Hartzell's Depression-era *Autumn Leaves* to the Chippewa County Piecemaker's 1990 hearts and stars design.

Scrap quilts are the happiest quilts of all. Their colors, prints, and patterns fairly dance across the surface of their tops. Go ahead, turn the pages and see if you don't find one that will make your fingers start dancing as well.

Happy stitching,

WORKSHOP

Selecting Fabrics

The best fabric for quilts is 100% cotton. Yardage requirements are based on 44"-wide fabric and allow for shrinkage. All fabrics, including backing, should be machine-washed, dried, and pressed before cutting. Use warm water and detergent but not fabric softener.

Necessary Notions

- Scissors
- Rotary cutter and mat
- Acrylic rulers
- Template plastic
- Pencils for marking cutting lines
- Sewing needles
- Sewing thread
- Sewing machine
- Seam ripper
- Pins
- Iron and ironing board
- Quilting needles
- Thimble
- Hand quilting thread
- Machine quilting thread

Making Templates

A template is a duplication of a printed pattern, made from a sturdy material, which is traced onto fabric. Many regular shapes such as squares and triangles can be marked directly on the fabric with a ruler, but you need templates for other shapes. Some quiltmakers use templates for all shapes.

You can trace patterns directly onto template plastic. Or make a template by tracing a pattern onto graph paper and gluing the paper to posterboard or sandpaper. (Sandpaper will not slip on fabric.)

When a large pattern is given in two pieces, make one template for the complete piece.

Cut out the template on the marked line. It is important that a template be traced, marked, and cut accurately. If desired, punch out corner dots with a ⅛"-diameter hole punch **(Diagram 1).**

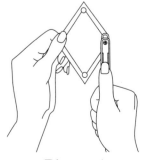

Diagram 1

Mark each template with its letter and grain line. Verify the template's accuracy, placing it over the printed pattern. Any discrepancy, however small, is multiplied many times as the quilt is assembled. Another way to check templates' accuracy is to make a test block before cutting more pieces.

Tracing Templates on Fabric

For hand piecing, templates should be cut to the finished size of the piece so seam lines can be marked on the fabric. Avoiding the selvage, place the template *facedown* on the *wrong* side of the fabric, aligning the template grain line with the straight grain. Hold the template firmly and trace around it. Repeat as needed, leaving ½" between tracings **(Diagram 2).**

Diagram 2

For machine piecing, templates should include seam allowances. These templates are used in the same manner as for hand piecing, but you can mark the fabric using common lines for efficient cutting **(Diagram 3).** Mark corners on fabric through holes in the template.

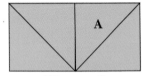

Diagram 3

For hand or machine piecing, use window templates to enhance accuracy by drawing and cutting out both cutting and sewing lines. The guidance of a drawn seam line is very useful for sewing set-in seams, when pivoting at a precise point is critical. Used on the right side of the fabric, window templates help you cut specific motifs with accuracy **(Diagram 4).**

Diagram 4

For hand appliqué, templates should be made the finished size. Place templates *faceup* on the *right* side of the fabric. Position tracings at least ½" apart **(Diagram 5).** Add a ¼" seam allowance around pieces when cutting.

Diagram 5

Cutting

Grain Lines

Woven threads form the fabric's grain. Lengthwise grain, parallel to the selvages, has the least stretch; crosswise grain has a little more give.

Long strips such as borders should be cut lengthwise whenever possible and cut first to ensure that you have the necessary length. Usually, other pieces can be cut aligned with either grain.

Bias is the 45° diagonal line between the two grain directions. Bias has the most stretch and is used for curving strips such as flower stems. Bias is often preferred for binding.

Never use the selvage (finished edge). Selvage does not react to washing, drying, and pressing like the rest of the fabric and may pucker when the finished quilt is laundered.

Rotary Cutting

A rotary cutter, used with a protective mat and a ruler, takes getting used to but is very efficient for cutting strips, squares, and triangles. A rotary cutter is fast because you can measure and cut multiple layers with a single stroke, without templates or marking. It is also more accurate than cutting with scissors because fabrics remain flat and do not move during cutting.

Because the blade is very sharp, be sure to get a rotary cutter with a safety guard. Keep the guard in the safe position at all times, except when making a cut. *Always keep the cutter out of the reach of children.*

Use the cutter with a self-healing mat. A good mat for cutting strips is at least 23" wide.

1. Squaring the fabric is the first step in accurate cutting. Fold the fabric with selvages aligned. With the yardage to your right, align a small square ruler with the fold near the cut edge. Place a long ruler against the left side of the square (**Diagram 6**). Keeping the long ruler in place, remove the square. Hold the ruler in place with your left hand as you cut, rolling the cutter *away from you* along the ruler's edge with a steady motion. You can move your left hand along the ruler as you cut, but do not change the position of the ruler. *Keep your fingers away from the ruler's edge when cutting.*

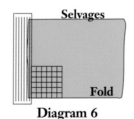

Diagram 6

2. Open the fabric. If the cut was not accurately perpendicular to the fold, the edge will be V-shaped instead of straight (**Diagram 7**). Correct the cut if necessary.

Correct cut   Not cut at 90° angle

Fold

Diagram 7

3. With a transparent ruler, you can measure and cut at the same time. Fold the fabric in half again, aligning the selvages with the fold, making four layers that line up perfectly along the cut edge. Project instructions designate the strip width needed. Position the ruler to measure the correct distance from the edge (**Diagram 8**) and cut. The blade will easily cut through all four layers. Check the strip to be sure the cut is straight. The strip length is the width of the fabric, approximately 43" to 44". Using the ruler again, trim selvages, cutting about 3/8" from each end.

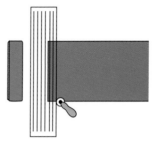

Diagram 8

4. To cut squares and rectangles from a strip, align the desired measurement on the ruler with the strip end and cut across the strip (**Diagram 9**).

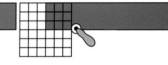

Diagram 9

5. Cut triangles from squares or rectangles. Cutting instructions often direct you to cut a square in half or in quarters diagonally to make right triangles, and this technique can apply to rectangles, too (**Diagram 10**). The outside edges of the square or rectangle are on the straight of the grain, so triangle sides cut on the diagonal are bias.

Diagram 10

6. Some projects in this book use a time-saving technique called strip piecing. With this method, strips are joined to make a pieced band. Cut across the seams of this band to cut preassembled units (**Diagram 11**).

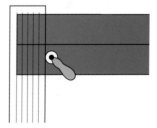

Diagram 11

Machine Piecing

Your sewing machine does not have to be a new, computerized model. A good straight stitch is all that's necessary, but it may be helpful to have a nice satin stitch for appliqué. Clean and oil your machine regularly, use good-quality thread, and replace needles frequently.

1. Patches for machine piecing are cut with the seam allowance included, but the sewing line is not usually marked. Therefore, a way to make a consistent ¼" seam is essential. Some presser feet have a right toe that is ¼" from the needle. Other machines have an adjustable needle that can be set for a ¼" seam. If your machine has neither feature, experiment to find how the fabric must be placed to make a ¼" seam. Mark this position on the presser foot or throat plate.

2. Use a stitch length that makes a strong seam but is not too difficult to remove with a seam ripper. The best setting is usually 10 to 12 stitches per inch.

3. Pin only when really necessary. If a straight seam is less than 4" and does not have to match an adjoining seam, pinning is not necessary.

4. When intersecting seams must align (**Diagram 12**), match the units with right sides facing and push a pin through both seams at the seam line. Turn the pinned unit to the right side to check the alignment; then pin securely. As you sew, remove each pin just before the needle reaches it.

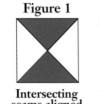

Figure 1   **Figure 2**

Intersecting seams aligned   Intersecting seams not aligned

Diagram 12

5. Block assembly diagrams are used throughout this book to show how pieces should be joined. Make small units first; then join them in rows and continue joining rows to finish the block (**Diagram 13**). Blocks are joined in the same manner to complete the quilt top.

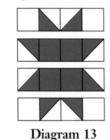

Diagram 13

6. Chain piecing saves time. Stack pieces to be sewn in pairs, with right sides facing. Join the first pair as usual. At the end of the seam, do not backstitch, cut the thread, or lift the presser foot. Just feed in the next pair of pieces—the machine will make a few stitches between pieces before the needle strikes the second piece of fabric. Continue sewing in this way until all pairs are joined. Stack the chain of pieces until you are ready to clip them apart (**Diagram 14**).

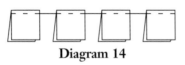

Diagram 14

7. Most seams are sewn straight across, from raw edge to raw edge. Since they will be crossed by other seams, they do not require backstitching to secure them.

8. When piecing diamonds or other angled seams, you may need to make set-in seams. For these, always mark the corner dots (shown on the patterns) on the fabric pieces. Stitch one side, starting at the outside edge and being careful not to sew beyond the dot into the seam allowance (**Diagram 15, Figure A**). Backstitch. Align the other side of the piece as needed, with right sides facing. Sew from the dot to the outside edge (**Figure B**).

9. Sewing curved seams requires extra care. First, mark the centers of both the convex (outward) and concave (inward) curves (**Diagram 16**). Staystitch just inside the seam allowance of both pieces. Clip the concave piece to the stitching (**Figure A**). With right sides facing and raw edges aligned, pin the two patches together at the center (**Figure B**) and at the left edge (**Figure C**). Sew from edge to center, stopping frequently to check that the raw edges are aligned. Stop at the center with the needle down. Raise the presser foot and pin the pieces together from the center to the right edge. Lower the foot and continue to sew. Press seam allowances toward the concave curve (**Figure D**).

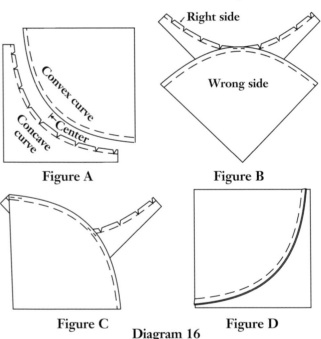

Figure A   **Figure B**

Figure C   **Figure D**

Diagram 16

Hand Piecing

Make a running stitch of 8 to 10 stitches per inch along the marked seam line on the wrong side of the fabric. Don't pull the fabric as you sew; let the pieces lie relaxed in your hand. Sew from seam line to seam line, not from edge to edge as in machine piecing.

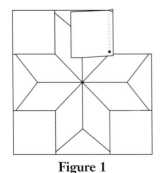

Figure 1   **Figure 2**

Diagram 15

When ending a line of stitching, backstitch over the last stitch and make a loop knot (**Diagram 17**).

Diagram 17

Match seams and points accurately, pinning patches together before piecing. Align match points as described in Step 4 under Machine Piecing.

When joining units where several seams meet, do not sew over seam allowances; sew *through* them at the match point (**Diagram 18**). When four or more seams meet, press the seam allowances in the same direction to reduce bulk (**Diagram 19**).

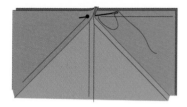
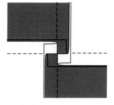

Diagram 18   **Diagram 19**

Pressing

Careful pressing is necessary for precise piecing. Press each seam as you go. Sliding the iron back and forth may push the seam out of shape. Use an up-and-down motion, lifting the iron from spot to spot. Press the seam flat on the wrong side. Open the piece and, on the right side, press both seam allowances to one side (usually toward the darker fabric). Pressing the seam open leaves tiny gaps through which batting may beard.

Appliqué

Traditional Hand Appliqué

Hand appliqué requires that you turn under a seam allowance around the shape to prevent frayed edges.

1. Trace around the template on the right side of the fabric. This line indicates where to turn the seam allowance. Cut each piece approximately ¼" outside the line.

2. For simple shapes, turn the edges by pressing the seam allowance to the back; complex shapes may require basting the seam allowance. Sharp points and strong curves are best appliquéd with freezer paper. Clip curves to make a smooth edge. With practice, you can work without pressing seam allowances, turning edges under with the needle as you sew.

3. Do not turn under any seam allowance that will be covered by another appliqué piece.

4. To stitch, use one strand of cotton-wrapped polyester sewing thread in a color that matches the appliqué. Use a slipstitch, but keep the stitch very small on the surface. Working from right to left (or left to right if you're left-handed), pull the needle through the base fabric and catch only a few threads on the folded edge of the appliqué. Reinsert the needle into the base fabric, under the top thread on the appliqué edge to keep the thread from tangling (**Diagram 20**).

5. An alternative to slipstitching is to work a decorative buttonhole stitch around each figure (**Diagram 21**).

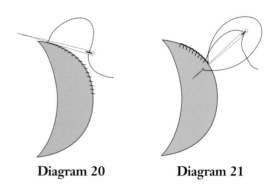

Diagram 20   **Diagram 21**

Freezer Paper Hand Appliqué

Supermarket freezer paper saves time because it eliminates the need for basting seam allowances.

1. Trace the template onto the *dull* side of the freezer paper and cut the paper on the marked line. *Note:* If a design is not symmetrical, turn the template over and trace a mirror image so the fabric piece won't be reversed when you cut it out.

2. Pin the freezer-paper shape, with its *shiny side up*, to the *wrong side* of the fabric. Following the paper shape and adding a scant ¼" seam allowance, cut out the fabric piece. Do not remove pins.

3. Using just the tip of a dry iron, press the seam allowance to the shiny side of the paper. Be careful not to touch the freezer paper with the iron.

4. Appliqué the piece to the background as in traditional appliqué. Trim the fabric from behind the shape, leaving ¼" seam allowances. Separate the freezer paper from the fabric with your fingernail and pull gently to remove it. If you prefer not to trim the background fabric, pull out the freezer paper before you complete stitching.

5. Sharp points require special attention. Turn the point down and press it (**Diagram 22, Figure A**). Fold the seam allowance on one side over the point and press (**Figure B**); then fold the other seam allowance over the point and press (**Figure C**).

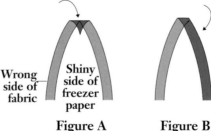

Wrong side of fabric   Shiny side of freezer paper

Figure A   **Figure B**   **Figure C**

Diagram 22

6. When pressing curved edges, clip sharp inward curves **(Diagram 23)**. If the shape doesn't curve smoothly, separate the paper from the fabric with your fingernail and try again.

Diagram 23

7. Remove the pins when all seam allowances have been pressed to the freezer paper. Position the prepared appliqué right side up on the background fabric. Press to adhere it to the background fabric.

Machine Appliqué

A machine-sewn satin stitch makes a neat edging. For machine appliqué, cut appliqué pieces without adding seam allowances.

Using fusible web to adhere pieces to the background adds a stiff extra layer to the appliqué and is not appropriate for some quilts. It is best used on small pieces, difficult fabrics, or for wall hangings and accessories in which added stiffness is acceptable. The web prevents fraying and shifting during appliqué.

Place tear-away stabilizer under the background fabric behind the appliqué. Machine-stitch the appliqué edges with a satin stitch or close-spaced zigzag **(Diagram 24)**. Test the stitch length and width on a sample first. Use an open-toed presser foot. Remove the stabilizer when appliqué is complete.

Diagram 24

Measuring Borders

Because seams may vary and fabrics may stretch a bit, opposite sides of your assembled quilt top may not be the same measurement. You can (and should) correct this when you add borders.

Measure the length of each side of the quilt. Trim the side border strips to match the *shorter* of the two sides. Join borders to the quilt as described below, easing the longer side of the quilt to fit the border. Join borders to the top and bottom edges in the same manner.

Straight Borders

Side borders are usually added first **(Diagram 25)**. With right sides facing and raw edges aligned, pin the center of one border strip to the center of one side of

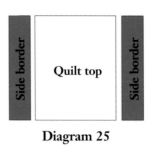

Diagram 25

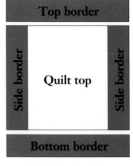

Diagram 26

the quilt top. Pin the border to the quilt at each end and then pin along the side as desired. Machine-stitch with the border strip on top. Press the seam allowance toward the border. Trim excess border fabric at each end. In the same manner, add the border to the opposite side and then the top and bottom borders **(Diagram 26)**.

Mitered Borders

1. Measure your quilt sides. Trim the side border strips to fit the shorter side *plus* the width of the border *plus* 2".

2. Center the measurement of the shorter side on one border strip, placing a pin at each end and at the center of the measurement.

3. With right sides facing and raw edges aligned, match the pins on the border strip to the center and corners of the longer side of the quilt. (Border fabric will extend beyond the corners.)

4. Start machine-stitching at the top pin, backstitching to lock the stitches. Continue to sew, easing the quilt between pins. Stop at the last pin and backstitch. Join remaining borders in the same manner. Press seam allowances toward borders.

5. With right sides facing, fold the quilt diagonally, aligning the raw edges of adjacent borders. Pin securely **(Diagram 27)**.

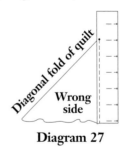

Diagram 27

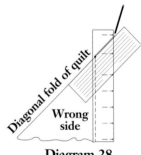

Diagram 28

6. Align a yardstick or quilter's ruler along the diagonal fold **(Diagram 28)**. Holding the ruler firmly, mark a line from the end of the border seam to the raw edge.

7. Start machine-stitching at the beginning of the marked line, backstitch, and then stitch on the line out to the raw edge.

8. Unfold the quilt to be sure that the corner lies flat. Correct the stitching if necessary. Trim the seam allowance to ¼".

9. Miter the remaining corners in the same manner. Press the corner seams open.

Quilting Without Marking

Some quilts can be quilted in-the-ditch (right along the seam line), outline-quilted (¼" from the seam line), or echo-quilted (lines of quilting rippling outward from the design like waves on a pond). These methods can be used without any marking at all. If you are machine quilting, simply use the edge of your presser foot and the seam line as a guide. If you are hand quilting, by the time you have pieced a quilt top, your eye will be practiced enough for you to produce straight, even quilting without the guidance of marked lines.

Marking Quilting Designs

Many quilters like to mark the entire top at one time, a practice that requires long-lasting markings. The most common tool for this purpose is a sharp **pencil.** However, most pencils are made with an oil-based graphite lead, which often will not wash out completely. Look for a high-quality artist's pencil marked "2H" or higher (the higher the number, the harder the lead, and the lighter the line it will make). Sharpen the pencil frequently to keep the line on the fabric thin and light. Or try a mechanical pencil with a 0.5-mm lead. It will maintain a fine line without sharpening.

While you are in the art supply store, get a **white plastic eraser** (brand name Magic Rub). This eraser, used by professional drafters and artists, will cleanly remove the carbon smudges left by pencil lead without fraying the fabric or leaving eraser crumbs.

Water- and **air-soluble marking pens** are convenient, but controversial, marking tools. Some quilters have found that the marks reappear, often up to several years later, while others have no problems with them.

Be sure to test these pens on each fabric you plan to mark and *follow package directions exactly.* Because the inks can be permanently set by heat, be very careful with a marked quilt. Do not leave it in your car on a hot day and never touch it with an iron until the marks have been removed. Plan to complete the quilting within a year after marking it with a water-soluble pen.

Air-soluble pens are best for marking small sections at a time. The marks disappear within 24 to 48 hours, but the ink remains in the fabric until it is washed. After the quilt is completed and before it is used, rinse it twice in clear, cool water, using no soap, detergent, or bleach. Let the quilt air-dry.

For dark fabrics, the cleanest marker you can use is a thin sliver of pure, white **soap.** Choose a soap that contains no creams, deodorants, dyes, or perfumes; these added ingredients may leave a residue on the fabric.

Other marking tools include **colored pencils** made specifically for marking fabric and **tailor's chalk** (available in powdered, stick, and traditional cake form). When using chalk, mark small sections of the quilt at a time because the chalk rubs off easily.

Quilting Stencils

Quilting patterns can be purchased as precut stencils. Simply lay these on your quilt top and mark the design through the cutout areas.

To make your own stencil of a printed quilting pattern, such as the one below, use a permanent marker to trace the design onto a blank sheet of template plastic. Then use a craft knife to cut out the design.

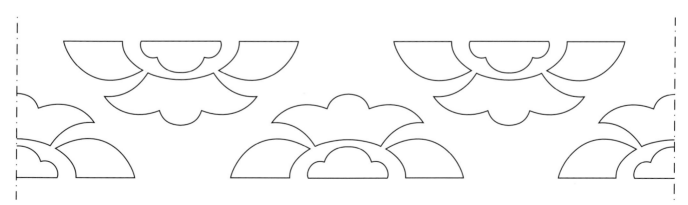

Quilting Stencil Pattern

Making a Quilt Backing

Some fabric and quilt shops sell 90" and 108" widths of 100% cotton fabric that are very practical for quilt backing. However, the instructions in this book always give backing yardage based on 44"-wide fabric.

When using 44"-wide fabric, all quilts wider than 41" will require a pieced backing. For quilts 41" to 80" wide, you will need an amount of fabric equal to two times the desired *length* of the unfinished backing. (The unfinished backing should be at least 3" larger on all sides than the quilt top.)

The simplest method of making a backing is to cut the fabric in half widthwise **(Diagram 29),** and then sew the two panels together lengthwise. This results in a backing with a vertical center seam. Press the seam allowances to one side.

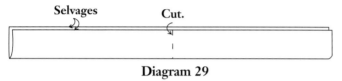

Diagram 29

Another method of seaming the backing results in two vertical seams and a center panel of fabric. This method is often preferred by quilt show judges. Begin by cutting the fabric in half widthwise. Open the two lengths and stack them, with right sides facing and selvages aligned. Stitch along *both* selvage edges to create a tube of fabric **(Diagram 30).** Cut down the center of the top layer of fabric only and open the fabric flat **(Diagram 31).** Press seam allowances to one side.

If the quilt is wider than 80", it is more economical to cut the fabric into three lengths that are the desired width of the backing. Join the three lengths so that the seams are horizontal to the quilt, rather than vertical. For this method, you'll need an amount of fabric equal to three times the *width* of the unfinished backing.

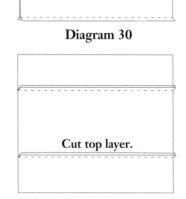

Diagram 30

Diagram 31

Cut top layer.

Fabric requirements in this book reflect the most economical method of seaming the backing fabric.

Layering and Basting

After the quilt top and backing are made, the next steps are layering and basting in preparation for quilting.

Prepare a large working surface to spread out the quilt—a large table, two tables pushed together, or the floor. Place the backing on the working surface wrong side up. Unfold the batting and place it on top of the backing, smoothing away any wrinkles or lumps.

Lay the quilt top wrong side down on top of the batting and backing. Make sure the edges of the backing and quilt top are parallel.

Knot a long strand of sewing thread and use a long (darning) needle for basting. Begin basting in the center of the quilt and baste out toward the edges. The basting stitches should cover an ample amount of the quilt so that the layers do not shift during quilting.

Machine quilters use nickel-plated safety pins for basting so there will be no basting threads to get caught on the presser foot. Safety pins, spaced approximately 4" apart, can be used by hand quilters, too.

Hand Quilting

Hand-quilted stitches should be evenly spaced, with the spaces between stitches about the same length as the stitches themselves. The *number* of stitches per inch is less important than the *uniformity* of the stitching. Don't worry if you take only five or six stitches per inch; just be consistent throughout the project.

Machine Quilting

For machine quilting, the backing and batting should be 3" larger all around than the quilt top, because the quilting process pushes the quilt top fabric outward. After quilting, trim the backing and batting to the same size as the quilt top.

Thread your bobbin with good-quality sewing thread (not quilting thread) in a color to match the backing. Use a top thread color to match the quilt top or use invisible nylon thread.

An even-feed or walking foot will feed all the quilt's layers through the machine at the same speed. It is possible to machine-quilt without this foot (by experimenting with tension and presser foot pressure), but it will be much easier *with* it. If you do not have this foot, get one from your sewing machine dealer.

Straight-Grain Binding

1. Mark the fabric in horizontal lines the width of the binding **(Diagram 32).**

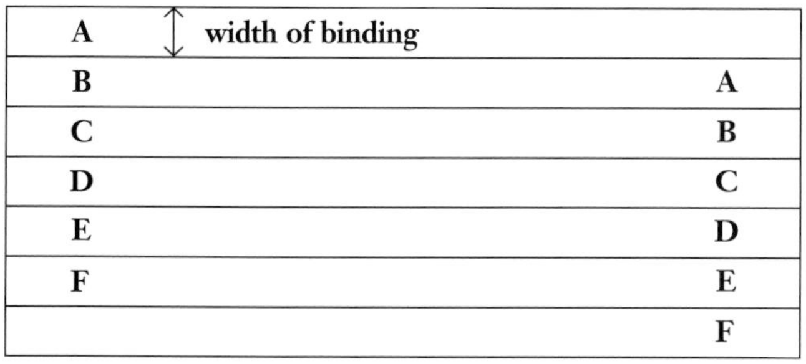

A	↕ width of binding	
B		A
C		B
D		C
E		D
F		E
		F

Diagram 32

2. With right sides facing, fold the fabric in half, offsetting drawn lines by matching letters and raw edges **(Diagram 33).** Stitch a ¼" seam.

3. Cut the binding in a continuous strip, starting with one end and following the marked lines around the tube. Press the strip in half lengthwise.

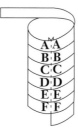

Diagram 33

Continuous Bias Binding

This technique can be used to make continuous bias for appliqué as well as for binding.

1. Cut a square of fabric in half diagonally to form two triangles. With right sides facing, join the triangles **(Diagram 34).** Press the seam allowance open.

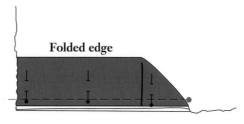

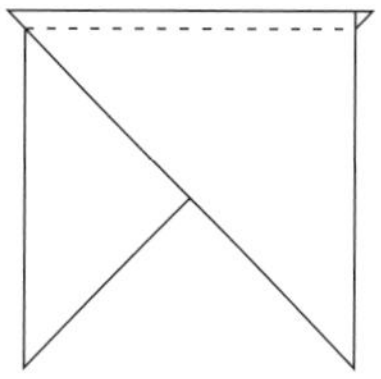

Diagram 34

2. Mark parallel lines the desired width of the binding **(Diagram 35)**, taking care not to stretch the bias. With right sides facing, align the raw edges (indicated as Seam 2). As you align the edges, offset one Seam 2 point past its natural matching point by one line. Stitch the seam; then press the seam allowance open.

Seam 2

Bias edge

Bias edge

Seam 2   Seam 1

Diagram 35

3. Cut the binding in a continuous strip, starting with the protruding point and following the marked lines around the tube **(Diagram 36).** Press the strip in half lengthwise.

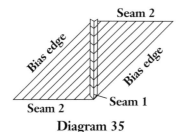

Seam 1

Seam 2

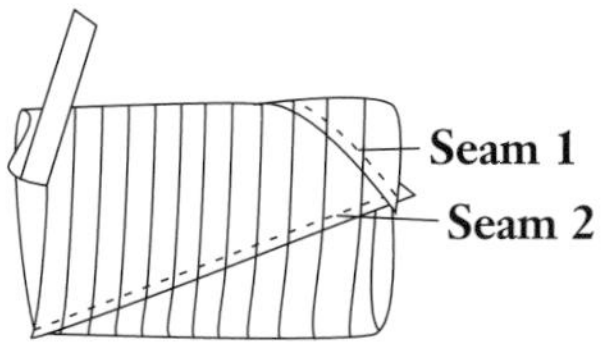

Diagram 36

Applying Binding

Binding is applied to the front of the quilt first. You may begin anywhere on the edge of the quilt except at the corner.

1. Matching raw edges, lay the binding on the quilt. Fold down the top corner of the binding at a 45° angle, align the raw edges, and pin **(Diagram 37).**

Folded edge

Diagram 37

2. Beginning at the folded end, machine-stitch the binding to the quilt. Stop stitching ¼" from the corner and backstitch. Fold the binding strip diagonally away from the quilt, making a 45° angle **(Diagram 38).**

3. Fold the binding strip straight down along the next side to be stitched, creating a pleat in the corner. Position the needle at the ¼" seam line of the new side **(Diagram 39).** Make a few stitches, backstitch, and then stitch the seam. Continue until all corners and sides are done. Overlap the end of the binding strip over the beginning fold and stitch about 2" beyond it. Trim any excess binding.

Front of quilt

Diagram 38

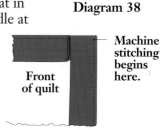

Machine stitching begins here.

Front of quilt

Diagram 39

4. Turn the binding over the raw edge of the quilt. Slipstitch it in place on the back, using thread that matches the binding. The fold at the beginning of the binding strip will create a neat, angled edge when it is folded to the back.

5. At each corner, fold the binding to form a miter **(Diagram 40).** Hand-stitch the miters closed if desired.

Back of quilt

Diagram 40

Quilt by Christine Schnaufer
Colona, Illinois

Judy's Star Surrounded

It's a whirligig of stars—a whirligig of colors, spinning and tumbling its way into your heart! Christine Schnaufer's scrap star quilt shouts with joy and makes you smile. Her star block is a modified version of Marsha McCloskey's Twisting Star* which is a variation of the Star of the Orient, designed by Judy Martin.** Christine added bars of color to the star and corner triangles to make a square.

*See McCloskey's *Pattern of the Month—Twisting Star* ©1985.
**See Martin's *Scrap Quilts*, Moon Over the Mountain Publishing Company, ©1985.

Finished Quilt Size

70" x 100"

Number of Blocks and Finished Size

70 blocks   10" x 10"

Fabric Requirements

Red print	1½ yards***
Green print	1½ yards***
Yellow print	1½ yards***
Orange print	1½ yards***
Blue print	1½ yards***
Navy print	1½ yards***
Lavender print	1½ yards***
Pink print	1½ yards***
Light scraps	1¼ yards total
Dark scraps	1¼ yards total
Muslin	5 yards***
Backing	6 yards

***Includes yardage for pieced bias binding.

Number to Cut#

Template A	70 muslin
Template B	560 muslin
	280 light scraps
	280 dark scraps
Template C	70 red print
	70 green print
	70 yellow print
	70 orange print
	70 blue print
	70 navy print
	70 lavender print
	70 pink print
Template D	280 muslin

#See Finished Edges before cutting fabric.

Quilt Top Assembly

1. Join all light scrap triangles (B) and dark scrap triangles (B) to muslin triangles (B) to form large triangles, as shown in **Block Piecing Diagram 1**. Join them to sides of octagon (A), alternating light and dark triangles. Begin at 1 edge of octagon and work to the left, as shown. To join last triangle, stitch up to the intersecting seam line of triangles and octagon. Stop and backstitch 1 or 2 stitches. Remove fabric from the machine. Align the remaining unstitched sides of triangles and stitch from the center to the outside edge.

2. Join trapezoids (C) to star, working to the right, as shown in **Block Piecing Diagram 2**. Arrange pieces in the color order shown and join pieces in the same order for every block made.

Join triangles (D) to corners of star to complete block, as shown in **Block Piecing Diagram 3**. Make 70 blocks.

3. Arrange blocks in 10 rows of 7 blocks each. (See quilt photograph on page 14.) Christine recommends placing the blocks on the floor or on a sheet to plan color arrangement. "I rotated blocks so that none of the same colors touched," says Christine.

Join blocks at sides to form rows and join rows.

Quilting

Outline-quilt ¼" inside seam line of all muslin pieces and trapezoids (C).

Finished Edges

To make Christine's pieced bias binding, follow instructions for Continuous Bias Binding on page 11 of the Workshop, with the following modification: Cut 2 (3½" x 51½") strips from the same fabrics used for trapezoid C. Cut 1 (3½" x 51½") strip from muslin. Join strips lengthwise in the color order shown in **Bias Strip Diagram 1** to make a 51½" square. Finger-crease and cut the square in half on its diagonal (bias),

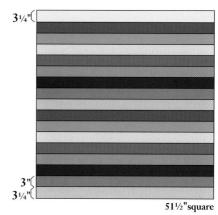

3¼"

3"
3¼"

51½"square

Bias Strip Diagram 1

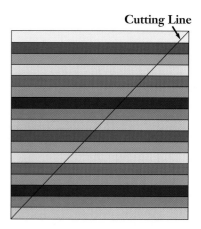

Cutting Line

Bias Strip Diagram 2

as shown in **Bias Strip Diagram 2**.

Remove long strip of muslin from first triangular piece. Leave the small muslin triangle attached to second triangular piece. Place triangular pieces right sides together, aligning long pink edge to long red edge at ¼" seamline. (See **Diagram 34** on page 11 of Workshop.) Stitch with ¼" seam to form a parallelogram. Open parallelogram and mark 2½" lines parallel to bias edges, as in **Diagram 35**, page 11. (Lines will run across colored strips.) Then, with right sides together and matching color strips, join Seam 2 edges to form a tube. (See **Diagram 36**, page 11.) Muslin triangle will be left free.

Cut a continuous bias strip, 2½" wide, beginning at the edge with the muslin triangle and going around and around until the whole tube has been used.

Join bias strip to quilt.

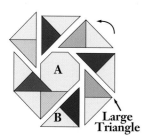

A

B   Large Triangle

Block Piecing Diagram 1

C

Block Piecing Diagram 2

D   D

D   D

Block Piecing Diagram 3

13

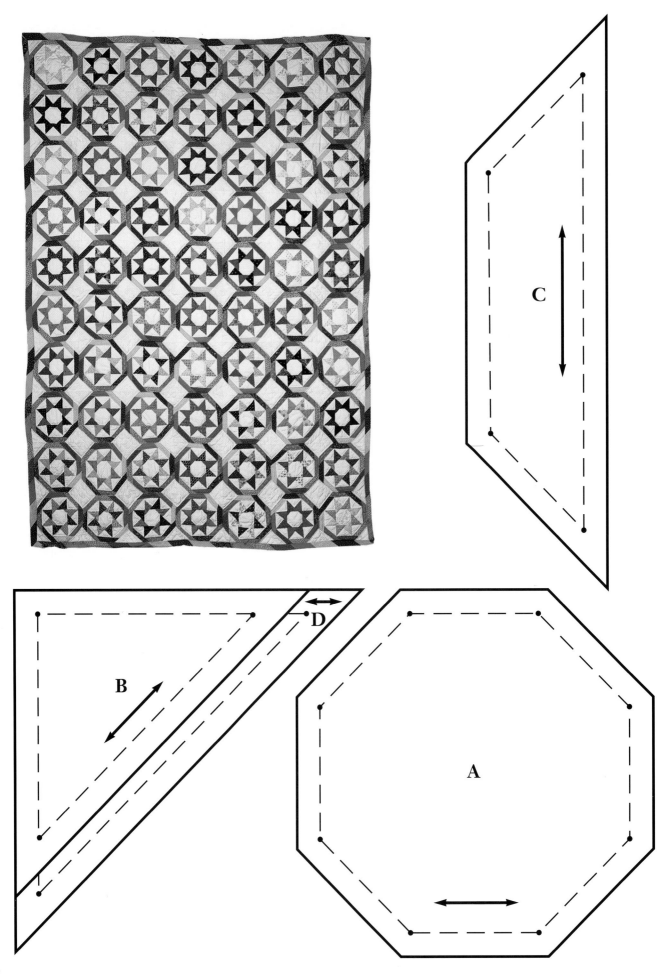

A

B

C

D

*Quilt by Scarlett Rose
Anderson, California*

Autumn Leaves

This interlocking leaf pattern has been popular with quilters since it was first introduced in a Nancy Page column in the 1920s. Scarlett Rose's version of this traditional favorite rounds up all the colors of autumn and pours them into one setting. The setting is barn-raising, which Scarlett borrowed from Log Cabin quilts. To make sure that the leaves are set correctly, she recommends that quilters carefully lay out their rows before assembling them. In addition, Scarlett appliquéd triangles in the borders to make every leaf complete. Each leaf is hand-quilted with a large leaf pattern.

Finished Quilt Size
95" x 95"

Number of Blocks and Finished Size
81 blocks   9" x 9"

Fabric Requirements
Green prints	1⅞ yards total
Orange prints	1⅞ yards total
Brown prints	1⅞ yards total
Yellow prints	1⅞ yards total
Red prints	1⅞ yards total
Black prints*	5¼ yards total
Backing	8¼ yards

*Select 2⅞ yards of 1 fabric and set aside for border. See Step 3.

Number to Cut
Template A	16 green prints
	16 orange prints
	16 brown prints
	17 yellow prints
	16 red prints
Template B	64 green prints
	64 orange prints
	64 brown prints
	68 yellow prints
	64 red prints
	18 black prints
Template C	16 green prints
	16 orange prints
	16 brown prints
	17 yellow prints
	16 red prints
Template D	156 black prints

Quilt Top Assembly

1. Arrange all pieces for inner quilt in rows, as shown in **Block Piecing Diagram** and **Setting Diagram 1**. (This is necessary to ensure proper color arrangement.) You will have 18 triangle Bs left over; these will be appliquéd to border in Step 3.

Pick up pieces in blocks and pin them together until ready for

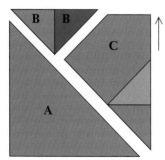

Block Piecing Diagram

assembly. Stack pinned blocks in order for each row and label rows. "It is important to keep them in order," says Scarlett, "since parts of each leaf (triangle Bs) extend into neighboring blocks."

2. Join block pieces, as shown in **Block Piecing Diagram**. Join blocks to form rows and join rows. (See **Setting Diagrams 1** and **2**.)

3. Cut 4 (7½"-wide) borders from 1 black print. Place each border right side up alongside each quilt edge. (Border corners will be mitered.) Align remaining triangles (B) with blocks, matching fabrics as shown in **Setting Diagram 2** and quilt photograph. With 1 raw edge of triangle aligned with raw edge of border, appliqué triangles to border. Join borders to quilt and miter corners.

Quilting
Quilt leaf pattern on page 18 in center of each block.

Finished Edges
Fold each square (D), as shown in **Prairie Point Folding Diagrams**. Arrange 39 prairie points in a continuous, overlapping fashion along each side of quilt, as shown in **Prairie Point Arrangement Diagram**. Baste prairie points together.

With right sides facing and raw edges aligned, stitch prairie points to quilt top, as shown in **Prairie Point Attachment Diagrams**. Turn under raw edge of quilt backing to cover raw edges of prairie points and blindstitch in place.

Prairie Point Folding Diagrams

Prairie Point Arrangement Diagram

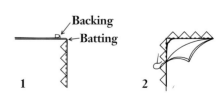

Prairie Point Attachment Diagrams

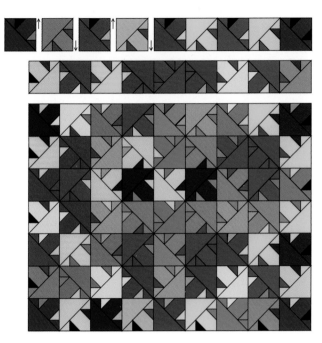

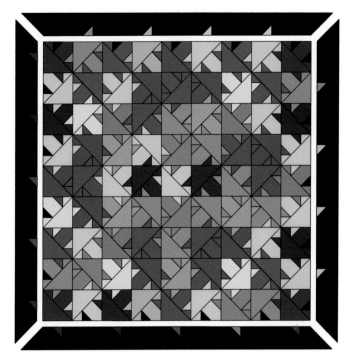

Setting Diagram 1

Setting Diagram 2

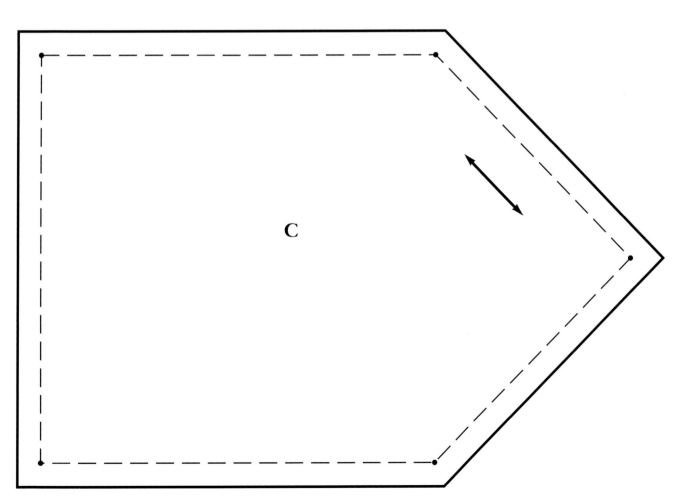

C

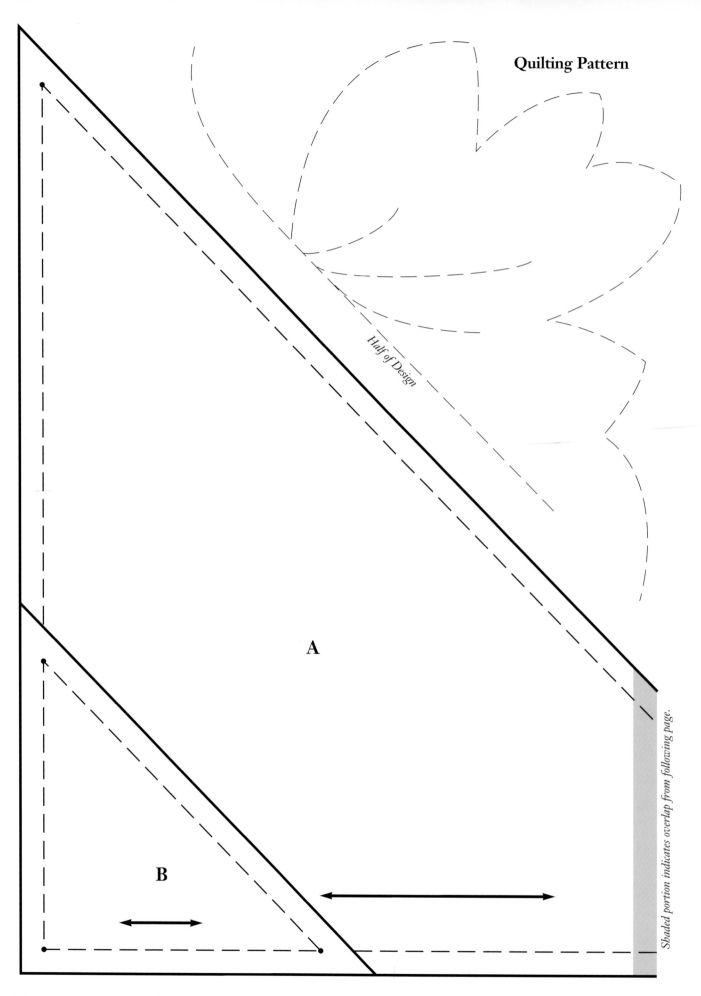

Quilting Pattern

Half of Design

A

B

Shaded portion indicates overlap from following page.

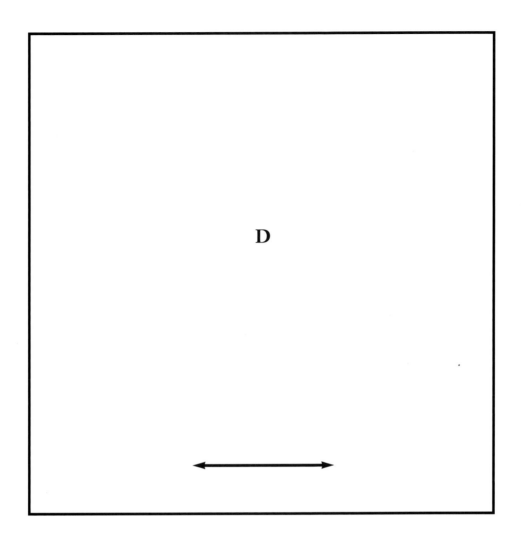

D

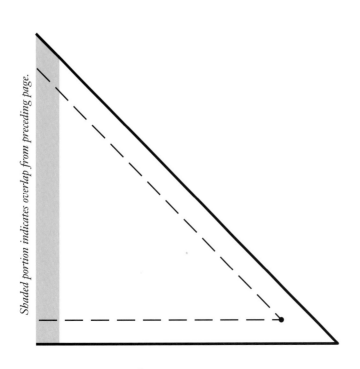

Shaded portion indicates overlap from preceding page.

Quilt by Karen Sikes Collins
Austin, Texas

Scrap Triangles

The patterns for a nine-patch scrap quilt are endless, as Karen Sikes Collins has learned. "This block so fascinated me that I have six quilts in mind, and the fourth is already pieced," she says. In this version, Karen's *Scrap Triangles #3,* sequencing light to dark scrap pieces and turning the blocks sends ripples of diamonds and pyramids radiating to the quilt's edge.

Finished Quilt Size

86" x 100"

Number of Blocks and Finished Size

168 blocks   7" x 7"

Fabric Requirements

Dark scraps   9 yards total
Medium scraps   6 yards total
Light scraps   3 yards total
Dark scrap for
   bias binding 1¼ yards
Backing   7½ yards

Number to Cut

Triangles*   1,512 dark colors
            1,008 medium
                colors
            504 light colors

*Before cutting, see Quilt Top Assembly, Step 1, for rotary cutter method.

Quilt Top Assembly

1. Cut scrap fabics into 3"-wide strips, either lengthwise or across the grain. Cut strips into 3" squares. Cut squares diagonally into 2 equal triangles until you have cut the required number. Or if you prefer, use triangle template and cut the number of triangles in Number to Cut.

2. Arrange triangles in sets of 9 dark, 6 medium, and 3 light triangles. Sew a dark triangle to a medium or light triangle along bias edge to form squares.

Arrange squares as shown in **Block Piecing Diagram**. (Arrow indicates the top of the block.) Join squares to form columns and join columns to complete block. Make 168 blocks.

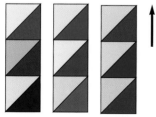

Block Piecing Diagram

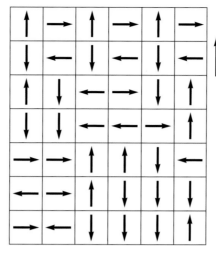

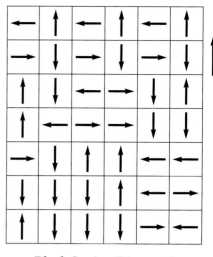

Block Setting Diagram 1 for a Quarter of Quilt (Make 2.)

Block Setting Diagram 2 for a Quarter of Quilt (Make 2.)

3. Arrange 6 blocks into 7 rows, as shown in **Block Setting Diagram 1 for a Quarter of Quilt**. (Arrows inside blocks indicate the top of each block. The arrow outside the diagram indicates the top of the quarter.) Stack rows before assembling. (Karen suggests running a thread through each stack twice to keep the blocks from turning.) Number each stack by row number to help with row assembly order. Join blocks at sides to form rows. Join rows to complete a quarter. Trim corners of triangles where they are bulky on back. Make 4 quarters, with 2 the mirror image of the others. (See **Block Setting Diagram 2 for a Quarter of Quilt**.)

4. Join quarters, as shown in **Setting Diagram**. Arrows indicate the tops of each quarter.

Quilting

To reinforce the strong diagonal lines of this quilt, outline-quilt ¼" inside seam lines of triangles.

Finished Edges

Bind with a continuous bias strip of dark scrap fabric.

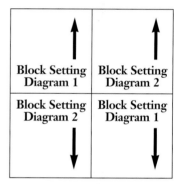

Setting Diagram

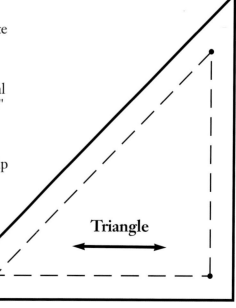

Triangle

Quilt by Chippewa County Piecemakers
Chippewa Falls, Wisconsin

Hearts of Chippewa

What more appropriate place to hang a quilt with hearts than in a cardiac rehabilitation center? No one can count the number of patients who must have felt a sense of caring and kindness from the presence of this quilt in the cardiac exercise and monitoring room. The quilt has since been raffled by the hospital and the group who made it, the Chippewa County Piecemakers. They are proud to say that enough money was raised to purchase a piece of exercise equipment for the center.

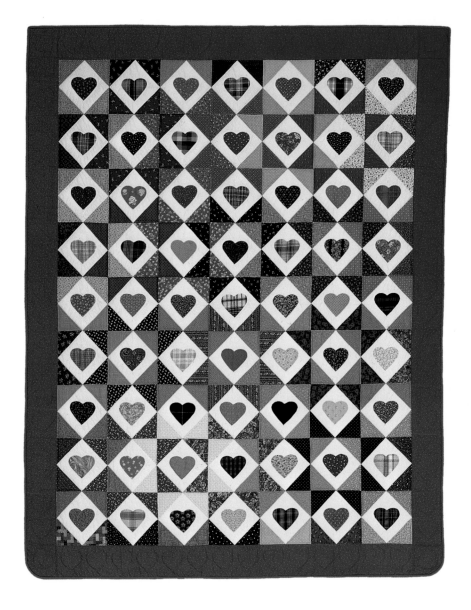

heart shapes and appliqué to muslin squares.

3. Alternate dark hearts with medium hearts and arrange squares in 9 rows of 7 squares each. (The Chippewa Piecemakers suggest laying out squares on the floor.)

Begin to "deal out" triangles to form a star around each heart, as shown in **Setting Diagram** and photograph. (Area within bold-lined square indicates how a star is formed with the triangles.) A dark heart will take a dark star, and a medium heart will take a medium star. (You will have triangles left over. The Chippewa Piecemakers felt that it was easier to cut 8 triangles from each fabric because you don't know which fabrics will be used until the hearts are made and arranged. Add the excess triangles to your scrap bag.)

Setting Diagram

Once completed, survey your arrangement and shift star sets if necessary. Try to keep colors evenly distributed to avoid clumps of color and to help each star show up distinctly.

4. Before stitching triangles to squares, tag each heart square with a block and row number to maintain proper order. Stitch triangles to corners of squares.

5. Join blocks at sides to form rows. Join rows.

6. Cut 2 (6½"-wide) borders from blue print and join to top and bottom of quilt.

7. Cut 2 (6½"-wide) borders from blue print and join to sides of quilt.

Finished Quilt Size
82" x 102"

Number of Blocks and Finished Size
63 blocks   10" x 10"

Fabric Requirements
Scraps*   6⅝ yards total
Muslin   5 yards
Blue print   3 yards
Blue for
  bias binding   1 yard
Backing   6 yards

*For triangles, a strip approximately 6" x 24" is needed from each of 26 dark fabrics and 24 medium fabrics. For hearts, a 6½" square is needed from each of 32 dark fabrics and 31 medium fabrics.

Other Materials
Freezer paper

Number to Cut
Triangle   400 scraps**

**Cut 8 triangles from each of 50 different fabrics. See Step 3.

Quilt Top Assembly
1. Cut 63 (7½") squares from muslin. Cut 63 (6½") squares from heart fabrics. (Cut 1 square per fabric.) Trace 63 hearts without seam allowance on dull side of freezer paper. Cut out hearts on traced lines.

2. Follow instructions on page 7 of Workshop to cut out fabric

Quilting

Quilt in-the-ditch around each heart and outline-quilt ¼" outside heart seam line. Quilt in-the-ditch of muslin and triangle seam lines. Outline-quilt ¼" inside and outside triangle seam lines.

For blocks that join side borders, quilt "missing" star points (triangles) at ends of alternating rows, beginning with Row 2. (See **Quilting Diagram**.) Quilt remainder of border with hearts, as shown.

Finished Edges

Trim border for round corners, as shown on quilt photograph. Bind quilt with bias binding made from blue fabric.

Quilting Diagram

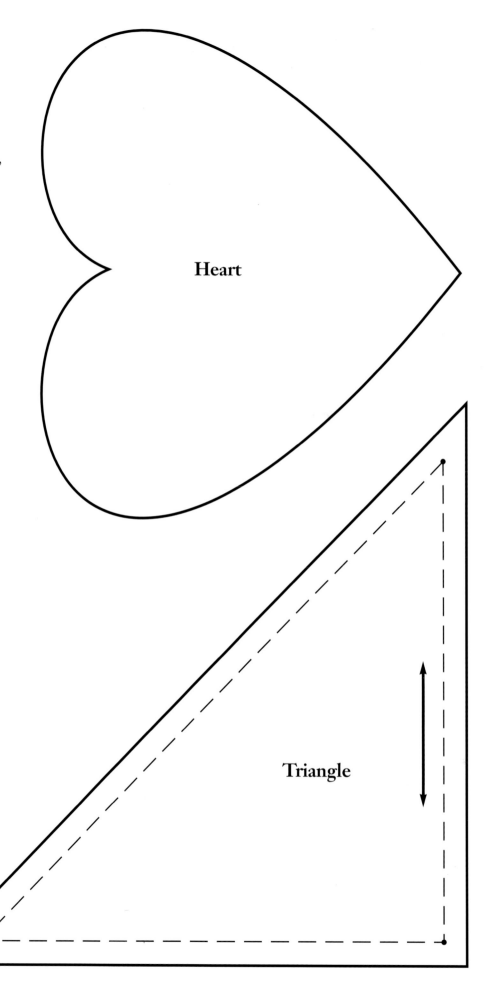

Heart

Triangle

Happy Hexagons

Sarah Jenkins wanted everyone around her to sleep warm and cozy, and she made several hundred quilts to make sure that they would. "My mother was completely willing to give a quilt to anyone who needed or wanted one. If someone's house burned, or if a wedding or shower came along, she would give a quilt. She just wanted everyone to keep warm," says Janie Shelby, Sarah's daughter.

Happy Hexagons, which Sarah pieced in her eighties, was one of the last quilts she made. It was quilted in a frame hanging from the ceiling and, like all of Sarah's quilts, was made entirely from scraps.

Finished Quilt Size
68" x 90"

Number of Blocks and Finished Size
56 blocks   10½" x 10½"

Fabric Requirements
Assorted solids   5¾ yards
Assorted prints   4½ yards
Pink solid   ¾ yard
Muslin for
  bias binding   1 yard
Backing   5½ yards

Number to Cut

Template A	364 assorted solids*
Template B	357 assorted prints**
Template C	63 assorted prints***
Template D	18 pink solid

*Cut 6 As of same fabric for each of 56 blocks and 4 As of same fabric for each of 7 half-blocks.

**Cut 6 Bs of same fabric for each of 56 blocks and 3 Bs of same fabric for each of 7 half-blocks.

***For each block, cut 1 C of same print as Bs.

Quilt Top Assembly

1. To make 1 Hexagon block, follow **Block Piecing Diagram** to join 6 As and 6 Bs. Appliqué 1 circle (C) to the center of block. Repeat to make 56 Hexagon blocks.

To make 1 half-block, join 4 As and 3 Bs as shown in **Half–Block Piecing Diagram**. Appliqué 1 C to center of half-block. Repeat to make 7 half-blocks.

2. Referring to **Setting Diagram**, join 8 blocks and 1 half-block to form 1 vertical row. Repeat to make 7 rows. Join rows and set in pieces (D) along sides as shown. Trim bottom pieces (D) even with edges of whole blocks. Trim edges of half-blocks even with edges of whole blocks.

Quilting
Quilt each seam in-the-ditch.

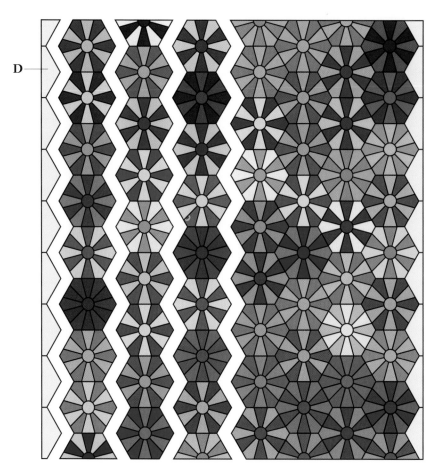

Setting Diagram

Finished Edges
Bind with bias binding made from muslin.

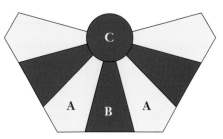

Half-Block Piecing Diagram

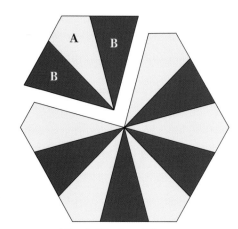

Block Piecing Diagram

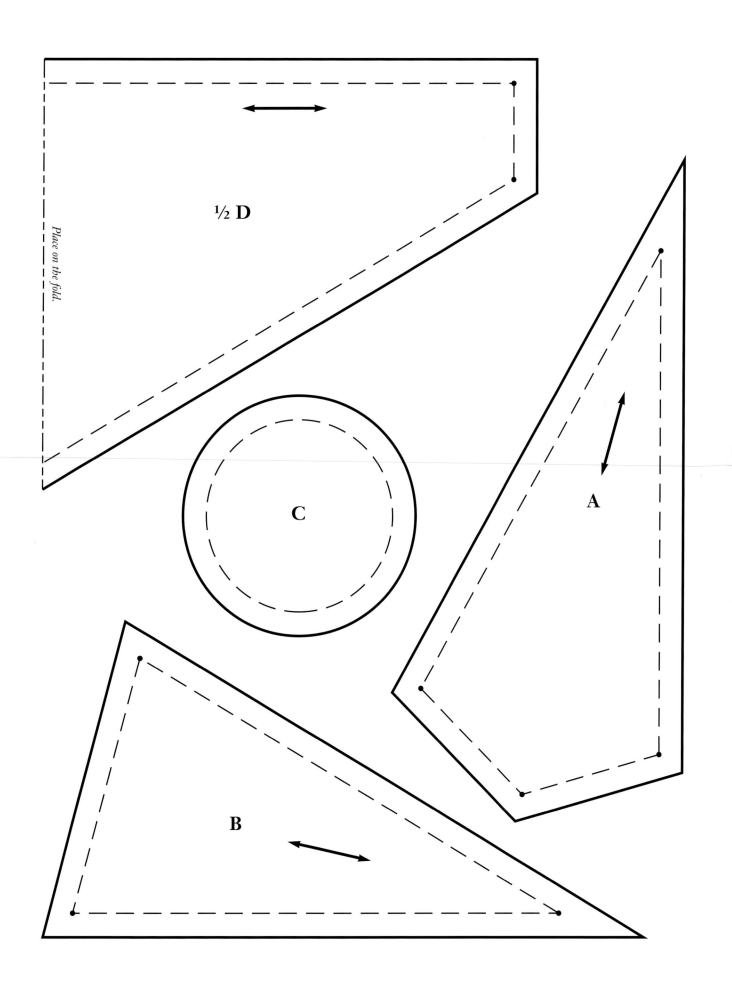

½ **D**

Place on the fold.

C

A

B

Quilt by the Golden Triangle Quilt Guild Beaumont, Texas

Spring Amish

Quilters from 23 neighboring Texas and Louisiana cities compose the membership of the Golden Triangle Quilt Guild. *Spring Amish* gloriously displays the precious scraps and stitches of 86 guild members. "I wanted a quilt that would get as many involved as possible," said quilt originator and project organizer, Anita Murphy. With so many members living in all directions from Beaumont, Texas, this design, based on a reversible quilt-as-you-go block, was ideal.

Finished Quilt Size

100" x 120"

Number of Blocks and Finished Size

120 reversible blocks   10" x 10"

Fabric Requirements

Pastel scrap
   prints   20 yards total
Blue print for
   piecing and
   binding   6½ yards
Muslin   8 yards

Quilt Top Assembly

1. Cut 60 (11") squares from blue print. Cut only 3 squares per row and save the leftover strip of fabric for binding. Cut squares along the diagonal to make 120 triangles.

2. Cut 60 (11") squares from muslin. Cut only 3 squares per row as before and save the leftover strip for sashing. Cut squares along the diagonal to make 120 triangles.

3. Cut 120 (11") squares of batting.

4. Cut 2 (1½"-wide) strips from scrap fabrics to go across the diagonal of the block. (Cut each with generous length that can easily be trimmed after attaching.) On the wrong side of each strip, mark a ¼" seam allowance on 1 edge.

5. Referring to **Block Piecing Diagram 1**, pin the blue print triangle to the front of a batting square and the muslin triangle to the back on the opposite end.

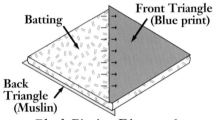

Block Piecing Diagram 1

Pin each scrap strip to the triangles (front and back), as shown in **Block Piecing Diagram 2**. Seam lines should match on both sides. Machine-stitch through the 5 layers. This is the hidden seam and must be accurate, or the rest of the block will be out of line.

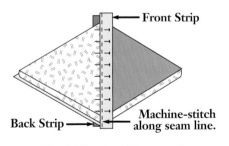

Block Piecing Diagram 2

6. Work on 1 side at a time. All strips are 1½" wide with seam allowance. (For our purposes, we will begin on the front.) On the front, finger-press the first strip toward batting. Pin second strip to first strip, batting, and back triangle. Be sure to pin the first strip on the back out of the way so it does not get caught in the second row of

stitching. (Anita recommends that you always finger-press strips before cutting the length. If you cut the strip before finger-pressing, it will be too short.)

Stitch through all 4 layers. This stitching will be the quilting for the back triangle so you may want to join these strips by hand. (Anita reminds you to stitch as straight a seam line as possible, so that your quilting rows on the back will be neat and straight.)

Add 8 strips in all in this manner to the front of the block.

7. Now turn to the back and repeat. Make 120 blocks.

8. Before setting blocks, make a master template 10½" square. Use this to trim blocks to a uniform size before joining.

Arrange blocks in 12 rows of 10 blocks each, as shown in quilt photograph. Cut 1 (2" x 10½") sashing strip from muslin. Fold in half lengthwise and press. With right sides facing and the muslin strip on top, join blocks together at sides. (See **Row Assembly Diagram 1**.) Appliqué folded free edge of muslin sashing strip to block, as shown in **Row Assembly Diagram 2**. Make 12 rows.

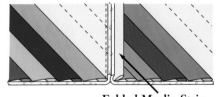

Folded Muslin Strip

Row Assembly Diagram 1

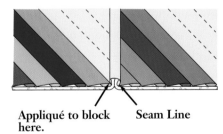

Appliqué to block here.   **Seam Line**

Row Assembly Diagram 2

9. Join rows with muslin strips the length of each row in the same manner as in Step 8.

Finished Edges

Bind edges of the quilt with blue print fabric.

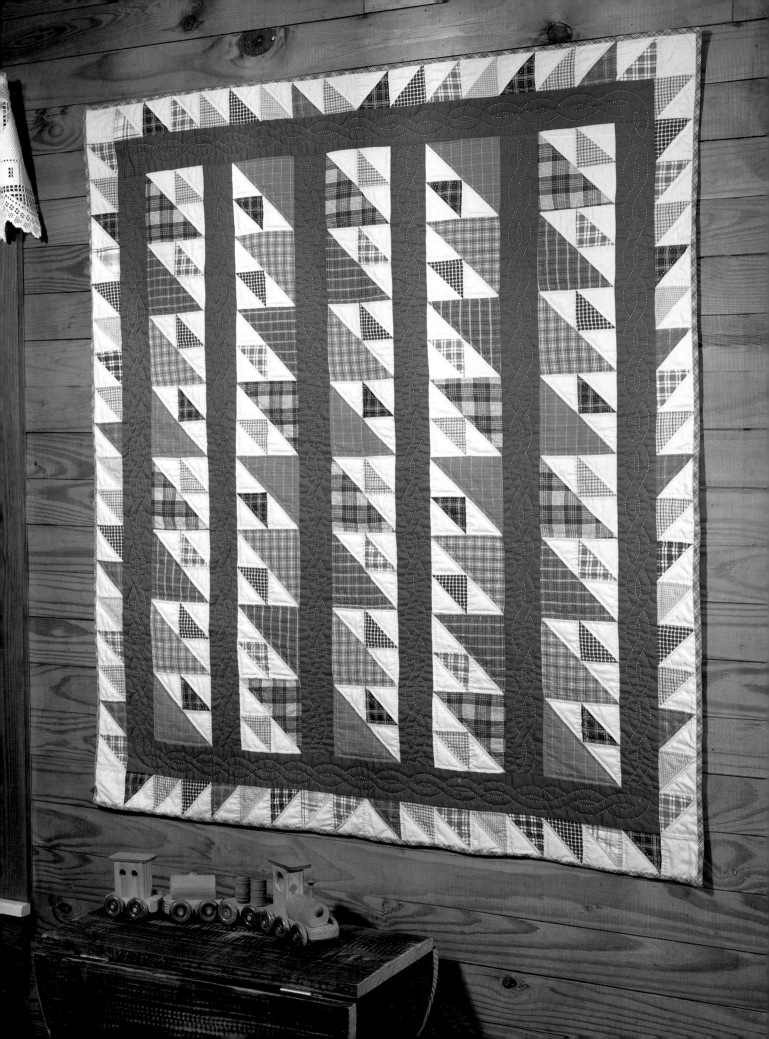

Vintage Plaids

Template-free! That's the way to go for Lois Richichi. Stimulated by the patterns of antique quilts, Lois challenges herself to figure out a method for duplicating them without using templates. "When you have a million quilting ideas rolling around in your head," she says, "template-free, machine-pieced quiltmaking is the only way to see them all through in a lifetime."

Vintage Plaids is Lois's adaptation of an antique quilt that used hundreds of plaids. She wanted to show her quilting class that the look of an antique quilt could be reproduced in a fraction of the time it would take using templates.

Finished Quilt Size
45" x 50"

Number of Blocks and Finished Size
40 blocks   5" x 5"

Fabric Requirements

Plaids*	1½ yards total
Muslin**	1¼ yards
Red	1⅜ yards
Plaid for bias binding	¾ yard
Ticking stripe for backing	3 yards

*At least ⅓ yard each of 4 different plaids is required.

**Use tea-dyed or unbleached muslin.

Quilt Top Assembly

1. Cut 1 (5⅞"-wide) strip across the grain from each plaid. Cut strips into 20 (5⅞") squares. Cut squares on the diagonal to make 40 triangles and set aside.

2. Cut a total of 5 (3⅜"-wide) strips across the grain from plaids. Cut 5 (3⅜"-wide) strips across the grain from muslin.

To make pieced squares, place 1 plaid strip and 1 muslin strip together with right sides facing. Draw vertical lines on muslin strip in 3⅜" increments, as shown in **Pieced Triangles Diagram**. Draw diagonal lines, as shown. Draw broken lines ¼" on each side of solid diagonal lines, as shown.

Pieced Triangles Diagram

Stitch on broken lines. Cut strips on all solid diagonal and straight lines. Repeat for other strips. Make 108 pieced squares and set aside.

3. Cut 4 (3⅜"-wide) strips from muslin. Cut 40 (3⅜") squares. Cut squares on the diagonal to make 80 triangles.

4. Join muslin triangles to sides of 40 pieced squares, as shown in **Block Piecing Diagram**. Join large triangles, cut in Step 1, to complete blocks, as shown.

Block Piecing Diagram

Quilt by Lois Richichi
Roslyn, Pennsylvania

5. Arrange blocks for color placement in 5 vertical rows before joining. Join blocks at sides, as shown in **Setting Diagram 1**.

6. Cut 6 (3"-wide) sashing strips from red. Alternate sashing with block rows, as shown in **Setting Diagram 1**. (Note that the direction of block rows is alternated.) Join rows to sashing.

7. Cut 2 (3"-wide) top and bottom sashing strips from red. Join to quilt, as shown in **Setting Diagram 1**.

8. Join 18 pieced squares for side border, as shown in **Setting Diagram 2**. Make 2 and join to opposite sides of quilt, as shown in **Setting Diagram 2**.

9. Join 16 pieced squares for top border, as shown in **Setting Diagram 2**. Repeat for bottom border. Cut 4 (3") squares from muslin. Join squares to opposite ends of borders, as shown. Join borders to quilt.

Quilting

Outline-quilt ¼" inside seam lines of all triangles. An unbroken cable is quilted on all sashing.

Finished Edges

Bind with plaid fabric.

Setting Diagram 1

Setting Diagram 2

Quilt by Mary Ann Keathley
Jacksonville, Arkansas

Hidden Circles

When someone spends much time and talent to achieve a goal, the satisfaction upon completion is often that much greater. That is probably why Mary Ann Keathley calls this her favorite quilt. *Hidden Circles* has been exhibited at several national shows. It won First Place in the scrap category at the 1990 Silver Dollar City Quilt Show in Missouri, and in the same year won Blue and Viewers' Choice ribbons at the Arkansas Quilter's Guild Show.

Finished Quilt Size

84" x 101"

Number of Blocks and Finished Size

32 blocks   12" x 12"

Fabric Requirements

Muslin	8 yards
Scraps	5 yards total
Print*	3⅛ yards
Green print	1¾ yards
Rust	⅛ yard
Light rust	⅛ yard
Backing	6 yards

*Includes yardage for border flowers, appliquéd border strip, and bias binding.

Number to Cut

Template A	142 scraps
Template B	142 scraps
Template B**	142 scraps
Template C	284 scraps
Template D	426 muslin***
Template E	142 scraps
Template F	142 scraps
Template G	132 muslin***
Template H	14 muslin***
Template H**	14 muslin***
Template I	28 muslin***
Template J	24 print
Template K	6 rust
Template L	6 light rust
Template M	10 green print#
Template M**	10 green print#
Template N	8 green print#
Template N**	8 green print#
Template O	16 green print#
Template P	16 print

**Flip or turn over template if fabric is 1-sided.

***See Step 4. Cut borders before cutting template shapes.

#See Step 5. Cut bias strips before cutting template shapes.

Other Materials

¼" and ½" metal bias bars

Quilt Top Assembly

1. Join pieces A through F to form a unit, as shown in **Block Piecing Diagram 1**.

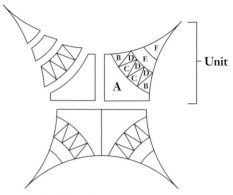

Block Piecing Diagram 1

Make 4 units for each block. Join 2 units at sides of piece As to form a section, as shown. Make 2 sections and join sections. Join piece Gs to sides of units, as shown in **Block Piecing Diagram 2**. Make 32 blocks.

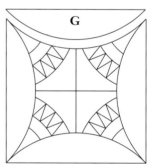

Block Piecing Diagram 2

2. Join pieces A through F and H to form a pieced square, as shown in **Setting Triangle Piecing Diagram**. Join 2 triangles (I) to sides of square to form a triangle, as shown. Make 14 pieced setting triangles.

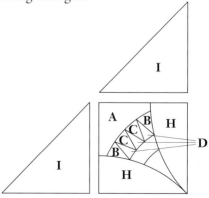

Setting Triangle Piecing Diagram

3. Join blocks at sides to form diagonal rows, as shown in **Setting Diagram 1**. Add piece Gs to 1 end of 2 rows as shown. Make 2 corner units. Join rows and corner units.

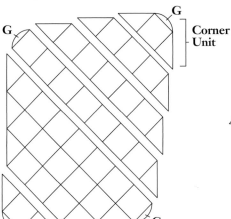

Setting Diagram 1

4. Cut 2 (8½" x 89") and 2 (8½" x 106") border strips from muslin. Join to quilt and miter corners, as shown in **Setting Diagram 2**. Leave corners square and trim after quilting.

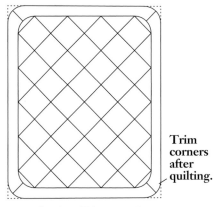

Setting Diagram 2

5. Cut 8 (⅞" x 30") bias strips from green print for vines. With right sides facing and raw edges aligned, stitch edges together lengthwise using ⅛" seam allowance. Use ¼" bias bar and steam-press strips with seam centered on back. Pin vines on border, as shown in quilt photograph, and appliqué in place.

Cut 4 (⅞"-wide) short bias strips for side flowers. (See quilt photograph.) Prepare strips as above.

Position flower petals (J) and stems at corners and sides of border and layer-appliqué, as shown in **Border Flower Piecing Diagram**. Layer-appliqué flower centers (K and L) to petals (J).

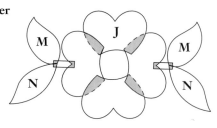

Border Flower Piecing Diagram

Gather 1 end of flower bud (P) under bud (O), as shown in **Bud Piecing Diagram**. Appliqué buds and remaining leaves (M and N) to vines, as shown. (Note that corner flowers do not have leaves [N]).

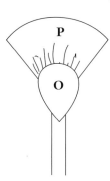

Bud Piecing Diagram

6. Make 9 yards (1⅜"-wide) continuous bias strip from print. Prepare strip as above in Step 5 but use ½" bias bar. Center over seam line of inner quilt and border and appliqué.

Quilting

Quilt in-the-ditch of seam lines of each unit. Outline-quilt ¼" inside seam lines of piece As. Quilt feathers in muslin pieces (G). Outline-quilt outside seam lines of all appliqué pieces and print border strip. Background-quilt diagonal lines, 1⅜" apart, in border.

Finished Edges

Use Template G to mark border for round corners. Join print bias binding to quilt, stitching on line for round corners. Trim excess fabric from corners, leaving ¼" seam allowance. Blindstitch binding to back.

Quarter of Design

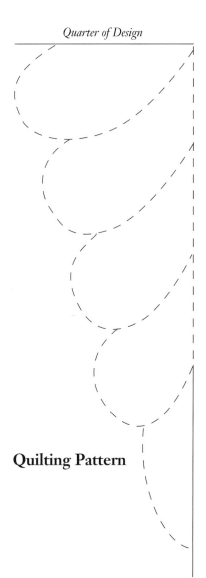

Quilting Pattern

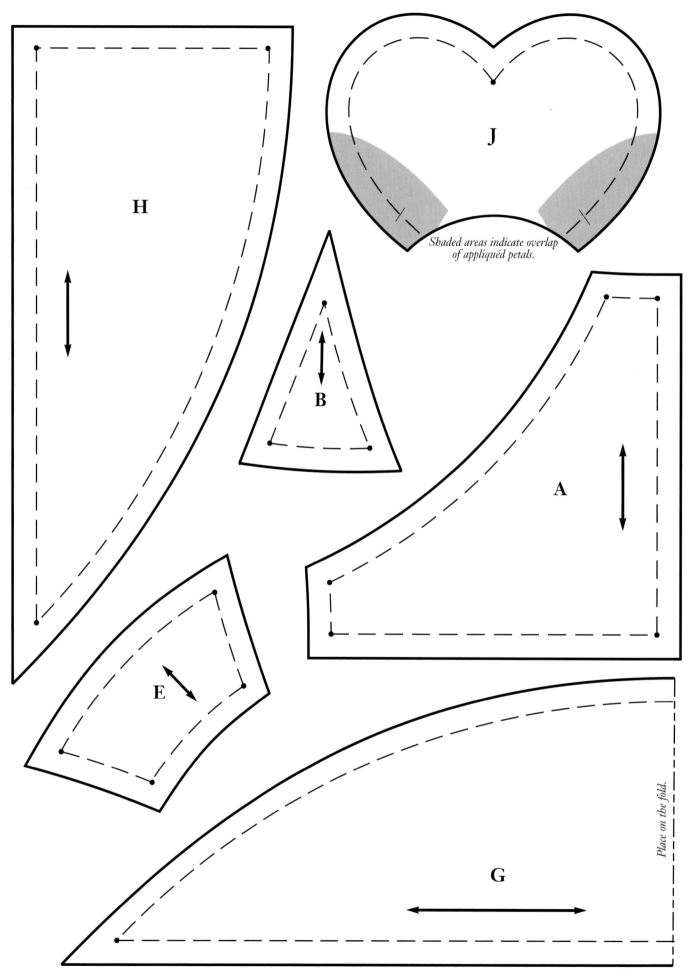

H

J

Shaded areas indicate overlap
of appliquéd petals.

B

A

E

G

Place on the fold.

Gather raw edge. Insert under piece O.

P

C

D

I

F

O

N

M

K

L

Quilt by Marie Thurston
Portsmouth, Rhode Island

Celebration

Marie Thurston made this wonderful quilt to commemorate retirement—"in celebration of all the time I now have," she says. Among other activities, Marie is a member of a quilt guild with a lovely name—Quilters by the Sea.

Marie loves to machine piece, and her *Celebration* will give you ample opportunity to polish your piecing skills.

Finished Quilt Size
80" x 90"

Number of Blocks and Finished Size
374 blocks   4" x 4"

Fabric Requirements
Light scraps   5¼ yards total
Dark scraps   5¼ yards total
Red for borders   2¾ yards
Navy print for
   bias binding   1¼ yards
Backing   5¾ yards

Number to Cut
Template   2,992 scraps*

*Cut 4 from light fabric and 4 from dark
 fabric for each block.

Quilt Top Assembly
1. Join 4 light and 4 dark pieces, as shown in **Block Piecing Diagram**, to make 1 block. Repeat to make 374 blocks.

2. Place blocks in 22 rows of 17 blocks each, reordering as necessary to obtain a pleasing color arrangement. Join blocks to form rows. Join rows.

3. Cut 2 (6½"-wide) border strips from red. Join to opposite sides of quilt. Cut 2 (6½"-wide) border strips from red. Join to top and bottom of quilt, butting corners. (Round corners after quilting is completed.)

Machine Quilting
Machine-quilt, outlining dark figure in each block with a continuous line of quilting. Then move to next block, until all blocks are quilted. Machine-quilt borders as desired.

Finished Edges
Using a plate or other round object of desired diameter, mark corners and trim. Bind with navy print fabric.

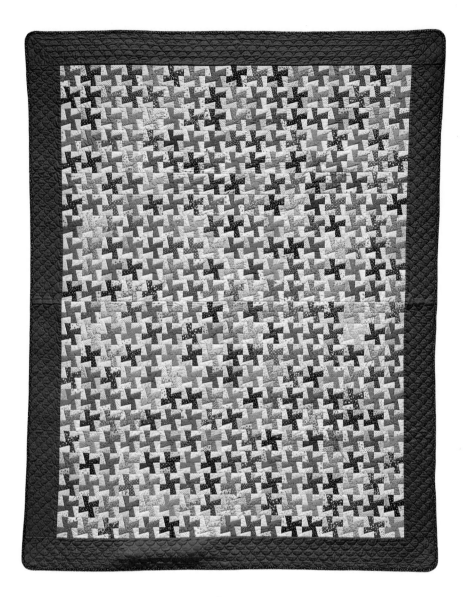

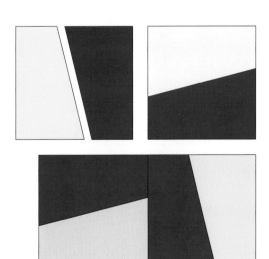
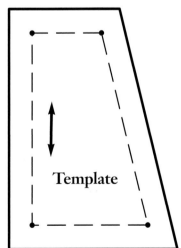

Block Piecing Diagram

Spring Beauties

Rosie Grinstead's *Spring Beauties* superbly captures the brilliance and freshness of spring, which bursts onto our landscapes after a gray winter. *Spring Beauties* has also captured the hearts of many quilt judges. It won Best Scrap Quilt and Color Award, National Quilting Association Show, 1989; First Place and Judge's Choice ribbons, Silver Dollar City Show, 1989; and Third Place in the Mid-Atlantic Quilt Festival II, Williamsburg, Maryland, 1991.

Rosie made the 36 blocks of *Spring Beauties* by setting four of Mary Ellen Hopkins's Buttercup blocks* together. Rosie used as many different prints as she could to make her 144 buttercups, but it isn't necessary to have 144 different fabrics. One pastel print, one beige print, and one green print are used for each buttercup, but the same prints can be used again in other buttercups.

*See Mary Ellen Hopkins's *The It's Okay If You Sit On My Quilt Book*. Atlanta, Georgia: Yours Truly, Inc., ©1982.

Quilt by Rosie Grinstead
Mission Hills, Kansas

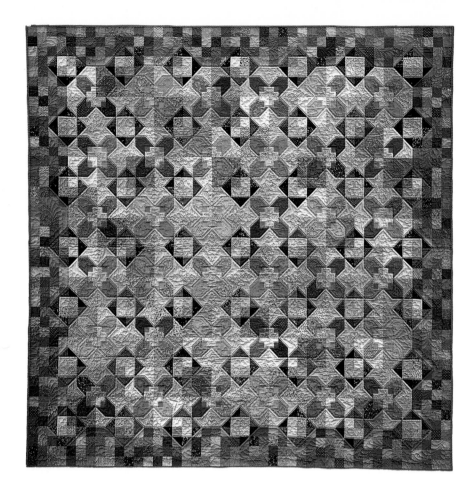

Quilt Top Assembly

1. Join pieces (A, B, C, and D), as shown in **Flower Block Piecing Diagram**. Make 28 blocks with peach flowers. Use 1 peach print, 1 beige print, and 1 green print for each block. Repeat and make 28 blocks each with yellow, blue, and pink print flowers. Make 32 blocks with lavender print flowers. This will give you a total of 144 flower blocks.

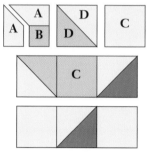

Flower Block Piecing Diagram

Join 4 flower blocks with the same color flowers, as shown in **Block Piecing Diagram**. Make 36 blocks.

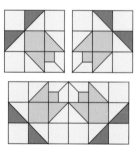

Block Piecing Diagram

2. Arrange blocks for the best color setting in 6 rows of 6 blocks each. Join blocks at sides to form rows and join rows.

3. Join squares (C) and triangles (D), as shown in **Border Segment Piecing Diagram**. (Use the same green print for the 2 triangles in each corner.) Make 24 segments.

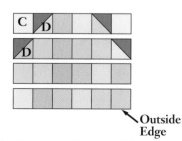

Border Segment Piecing Diagram

Finished Quilt Size
88" x 88"

Number of Blocks and Finished Size
36 blocks   12" x 12"

Fabric Requirements

Beige prints	4⅞ yards total
Green prints	1½ yards total
Peach prints*	½ yard total
Yellow prints*	½ yard total
Blue prints*	½ yard total
Pink prints*	½ yard total
Lavender prints*	½ yard total
Pastel prints**	2¾ yards total
Peach	⅛ yard
Yellow	⅛ yard
Blue	⅛ yard
Pink	⅛ yard
Lavender	⅛ yard
Blue print for bias binding	1¼ yards
Backing	7½ yards

 *For pieced flowers in blocks
**For borders

Number to Cut

Template A	144 beige prints
Template A***	144 beige prints
Template B	28 peach
	28 yellow
	28 blue
	28 pink
	32 lavender
Template C	28 peach prints#
	28 yellow prints#
	28 blue prints#
	28 pink prints#
	32 lavender prints#
	484 beige prints
	484 pastel prints
Template D	56 peach prints#
	56 yellow prints#
	56 blue prints#
	56 pink prints#
	64 lavender prints#
	576 beige prints
	392 green prints
	104 pastel prints

***Flip or turn over template if fabric is 1-sided.

#Use 1 fabric for each flower (1 C and 2 Ds).

4. Make 4 corner blocks, as shown in **Corner Block Piecing Diagram**. (Use a single green print for triangles in each corner block.)

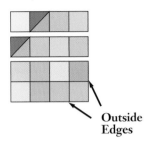

Outside Edges

Corner Block Piecing Diagram

5. Join 6 segments at sides 4 times each to make 4 borders, as shown in **Setting Diagram**. Join borders to top and bottom of quilt, as shown. Join corner blocks to opposite ends of remaining borders. Join borders to quilt.

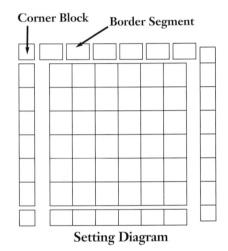

Corner Block   Border Segment

Setting Diagram

Quilting

Outline-quilt ¼" outside seam lines, as shown in **Quilting Diagram**. Quilt feather and heart patterns, as shown.

Finished Edges

Bind with blue print fabric.

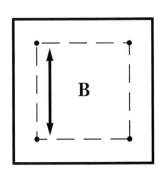

Quilting Diagram

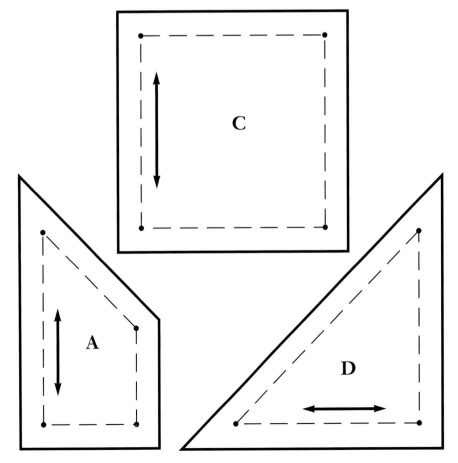

Evening Star

This quilt represents a quartet of quilters and a span of four generations. When Jennifer Rozens decided she wanted to learn to quilt, she remembered the little box of her great-grandmother's scraps stored in her mom's attic. She found, to her surprise and delight, that the box contained not just scraps, but dozens and dozens of quilt blocks.

As her introduction to quiltmaking, Jennifer chose the Evening Star blocks in the box and carefully hand-pieced and hand-quilted *Evening Star*. Since then, she has made a second quilt. "These quilts are my family," says Jennifer, "my history, and my reason for being proud to be a quilter."

Finished Quilt Size
56" x 65"

Number of Blocks and Finished Size
120 blocks   4½" x 4½"

Fabric Requirements
Plaids	2 yards
Muslin	2½ yards
Navy for border	1¾ yards
Pink for bias binding	1 yard
Backing	4 yards

Number to Cut
Template A	120 plaids
Template B	960 plaids
	480 muslin
Template C	480 muslin

Quilt Top Assembly
1. Join triangles (B) to squares (A and C), as shown in **Block Piecing Diagram**. Make 120 blocks.

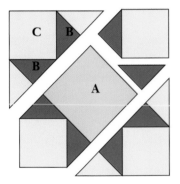

Block Piecing Diagram

2. Join blocks at sides in 12 rows of 10 blocks each. (See quilt photograph.) Join rows.

3. Cut 2 (6"-wide) borders from navy. Join to opposite sides of quilt. Cut 2 (6"-wide) borders from navy. Join to top and bottom of quilt.

Quilting
Quilt patchwork area in a 1" cross-hatching pattern. The navy border is quilted with an unbroken cable.

Finished Edges
Bind with pink fabric.

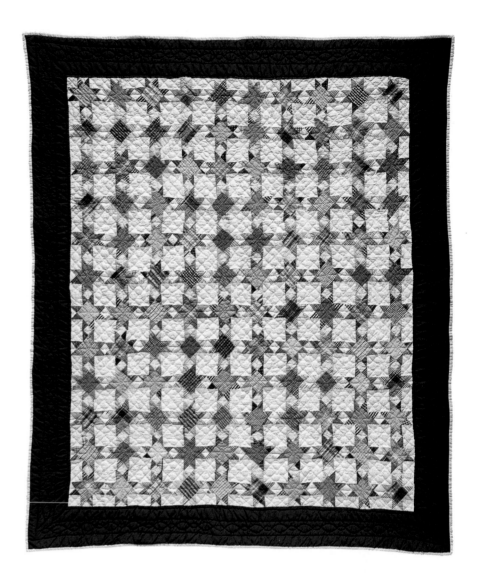

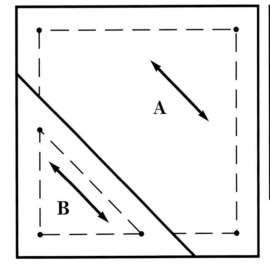

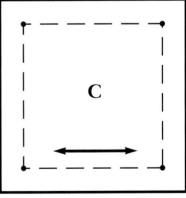

Quilt by Mary Eleanor Keller, Mary Elizabeth Brading, Nancy Keller, and Jennifer C. Rozens Arrowsmith, Illinois, and St. Clair Shores, Michigan

Autumn Leaves

Frequently, neighbors dropped in to visit Anna Hartzell when she was quilting. She was known for her quilting and her wonderful coffee. One visit by a young teenager named Milly Splitstone and her aunt proved to be a most special occasion. Anna was working on her *Autumn Leaves* quilt on that day, and Milly was immediately taken by the beauty of it. It was the first quilt with hand stitching that she had ever seen.

The impressions made on Milly that day inspired her to try quilting several years later. Today, she is also a quilt teacher and judge. In 1976, Milly was thrilled to have the opportunity to buy *Autumn Leaves* from a neighbor who cared for Anna in her last years. "People seldom have a chance to own the first quilt they ever saw," says Milly.

The *Autumn Leaves* pattern that captured Anna's and Milly's imaginations was readily available commercially in the 1930s and 1940s. Its popularity increased when it was seen at the Chicago World's Fair in 1933 at a quilt competition sponsored by Sears, Roebuck and Company.

For an entirely different treatment of the autumn theme, turn to page 15. There you'll see how a Nancy Page pattern from the 1920s inspired Scarlett Rose's version of *Autumn Leaves*.

Quilt by Anna Hartzell, Fremont, Michigan
Owned by Milly Splitstone

Finished Quilt Size
82" x 89"

Fabric Requirements
Prints   3¼ yards total
Pink   2 yards
Green   1¼ yards*
Muslin   4½ yards
Pink for
    bias binding   1¼ yards
Backing   7⅝ yards

*Approximately 35 yards of ¼"-wide
 (finished width measurement) bias
 binding are needed for vine and stems.

Number to Cut
Leaf   634 prints

Quilt Top Assembly

1. Cut 1 (25" x 32") rectangle
from muslin for center. Arrange
vines, stems, and leaves on rectangle, as shown in quilt photograph
and **Setting Diagram**. Pin in place
and appliqué.

Setting Diagram

2. Cut 2 (4½"-wide) borders
from pink and join to top and
bottom of quilt. Cut 2 (4½"-wide)
borders from pink and join to sides
of quilt.

3. Cut 2 (10½"-wide) borders
from muslin and join to top and
bottom of quilt. Cut 2 (10½"-
wide) borders from muslin and join
to sides of quilt. Pin vine, stems,
and leaves on muslin, as shown in
quilt photograph, and appliqué.

4. Cut 2 (4½"-wide) borders
from pink and join to top and
bottom of quilt. Cut 2 (4½"-wide)
borders from pink and join to sides
of quilt.

5. Cut 2 (11¼"-wide) borders
from muslin and join to top and
bottom of quilt. Cut 2 (11¼"-
wide) borders from muslin and join
to sides of quilt. Pin vine, stems,
and leaves on muslin, as shown in
quilt photograph, and appliqué.
(Appliquéing can also be done
before joining borders to quilt.)

Quilting
Anna quilted an overall clamshell
pattern on the entire quilt.

Finished Edges
Bind with pink fabric.

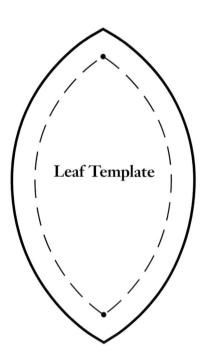

Leaf Template